Peacemaking Skills for Little Kids

Student Activity Book

by

Fran Schmidt
Alice Friedman
Elyse Brunt
Teresa Solotoff

James A. Burke II, Editor
Educational Editors, Nancy Mannion Brice and Catherine H. Diekman
Ron Dilley and Juanita Mazzarella, Graphic Designers
Cover Design by Linda Bladholm, Tracey Flanagan and Teresa Solotoff
Illustrations by Mario Baert, Linda Bladholm and Teresa Solotoff

PEACE WORKS
Peace Education
FOUNDATION

ISBN # 1-878227-49-1

I'M GLAD TO BE ME

I look in the mirror
And what do I see,
I see the me
No one else can be.

I am precious,
I am glad to be me,
My hair, my face,
My personality.

My size, my shape,
The color of my skin,
All make up me
Outside and in.

Draw your face in the mirror.

I'm glad to be me because _____

_____

My name is _____

And I really care.

I have _____ eyes

And I have _____ hair.

My skin is _____

And I'm _____ inches tall.

I look good, and that's not all!

I have _____ people in my family.

I love _____ and _____ loves me.

I like to play _____ with my friends.

I like to _____ when the day ends.

I would make _____ if I could cook.

_____ is my favorite book.

That's enough about me. This is the end.

Tell me about you, and make a new friend!

After you
fill in the blanks-
Say it as a rap !

I CARE !

Peacemakers care about themselves.

Making Friends

I have friends. This is how I make a friend.

1. I look at the person.

2. I smile.

3. I say:

Draw yourself with a friend.

Hello, my name is
_____
What is your name?

My name is
_____

A Friend Is...
Someone Who Cares And Shares

Some ways I am a friend are

_____

_____

_____

_____

 **Peacemakers like to meet new friends.**

Color each picture that shows good listening.

WE LISTEN

Look at each other.

Talk at the same time.

Ask questions if you don't understand.

Do something else when someone is talking to you.

TO EACH OTHER

Listen without interrupting.

Pay attention.

YES OR NO?

Can we listen if we are running around the room? _____

Can we listen if someone interrupts? _____

Can we listen if we are yelling? _____

It is important to listen to each other because _____

_____

When someone listens to me I feel _____

_____

Peacemakers show they care when they listen to each other.

Sounds In

I listen to the sounds in
MY ENVIRONMENT.

Write sounds made by nature.

Write sounds made by machines.

My Environment

Put a red circle around sounds made by machines. Put a green circle around sounds made by nature.

My favorite sounds are _____

_____

Peacemakers listen to the sounds in their environment.

HANDS ARE FOR HELPING

Color the pictures that show "Helping Hands".

I can help me, I can help you

That is what my hands can do.

I can hold the door open for you

That is what my hands can do.

I can pick up something for you

That is what my hands can do.

You can meet me, I can meet you

That is what my hands can do.

NOT HURTING

Draw your hands. On your left hand write some good things you do in school. On your right hand write some good things you do at home.

Peacemakers use their hands for helping, not hurting.

WORKING TOGETHER...
THAT'S COOPERATION

THIS JOB'S TOO BIG FOR ME.

THIS JOB'S TOO BIG FOR YOU.

BUT WE CAN WORK TOGETHER,

UNTIL THE JOB IS THROUGH.

Here is how I cooperate at home. _____

_____

_____

Here is how I cooperate in the classroom. _____

_____

_____

Here is how I cooperate on the playground. _____

_____

_____

Peacemakers cooperate to help get the job done.

We Can Work Together

Everyone has a job to do
Other people depend on you.
Everyone has a part to play
Working together is the best way.

What are some games you can't play alone?

_____

_____

_____

What do you like about playing with others?

_____

_____

_____

These children need help.

How can these children work together to clean this room?

_____

_____

Peacemakers work together to get a job done.

WHAT CAN I SAY ?

❤ We treat people with respect.

❤ Respect means caring about each other.

❤ I-Care Language tells other people that we care about them and their feelings.

Write the caring words in each balloon.

I'm sorry.

Excuse me.

Would you like a cookie?

May I please use your crayons?

Thank you for sharing.

Come and play with us.

I CAN SAY THE RIGHT THING

Peacemakers use caring words to show respect.

Body Talk

I can tell how people feel by looking at their body language.

Choose a word that shows how each is feeling.

_____   _____   _____   _____

_____   _____   _____   _____

Draw a picture showing how your body looks when you are happy...

afraid

happy

angry

lonely

excited

and when you are angry.

loving

sad

proud

Peacemakers know that body language shows feelings.

We're All A Family

All over the world there are boys and girls, just like me.

They work and play and learn together, just like me.

The children of the world belong

To one big family–

The human family.

Draw a picture of your family.

My family is special because _____

_____

_____

Under One Sky

We are different - not the same,
Different languages, different names.
From different places around the globe,
Different dreams, different hopes.
Yet we share our special earth,
This precious planet of our birth.
We are one family under one sky,
Let's celebrate our common tie.

> Find hello in different languages.

```
J A M B O T D V B S A
H B O H H H O G A S P
S H A L O M B N D D J
Y S A L A M R H O L A
X B A M W O E G N M Y
V F T V Z L D I I A M
N L B I B S E H H X P
M U U S Y X N C A O N
S Z V S B O N J O U R
L H E L L O Y Z M O R
```

HELLO	(English)	NIHAO	(Chinese)
JAMBO	(Swahili)	SHALOM	(Hebrew)
BON JOUR	(French)	DOBRE DEN	(Russian)
HOLA	(Spanish)	BONJOU	(Creole)

Peacemakers know that everyone belongs to the human family.

G R O W I N G

Nothing ever stays the same, things keep changing.

When I was a baby

I couldn't do

Much for myself,

I needed you

To help me eat

To tickle my feet

To wipe my tears

To calm my fears.

When I was a baby

The world was new,

Thank goodness,

I had you.

When I was a baby, I could

_____

_____

_____

CHANGING

As I started to change

And my body grew,

I learned to do

Many things brand new.

Tie my shoe

Count to two

Catch the ball

Get up when I fall.

I know there's more

I need to know,

As I get older

And continue to grow.

Draw yourself doing something you just learned.

Now that I am _____ *years old, I can*

_____

_____

Peacemakers become more capable and responsible every day.

KNOW YOURSELF
Inside and Out

Identify these body parts.

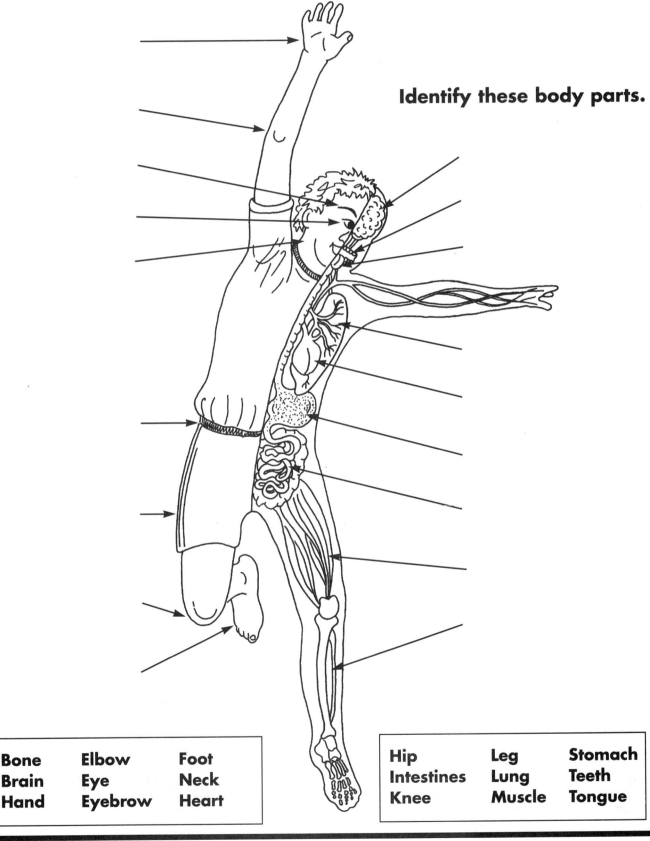

Bone	Elbow	Foot
Brain	Eye	Neck
Hand	Eyebrow	Heart

Hip	Leg	Stomach
Intestines	Lung	Teeth
Knee	Muscle	Tongue

Making Healthy Choices

Watching television all day

Circle the healthy choices.

Brushing your teeth

Riding in a car without wearing a seat belt

Crossing the street without looking for cars

Getting a good night's sleep

Taking a bath or shower every day

Sticking your arm out of the school bus

Eating healthy snacks

Wearing a bicycle helmet

Eating too much candy

Playing sports

DO YOU KNOW
where each food goes?

Put the following foods into the correct category.

chicken	cucumber	candy	cheese
french fries	potato	roll	nuts
hamburger	yogurt	crackers	black beans
eggs	ice cream	chocolate	peanut butter
peach	cake	cereal	sunflower seeds

Meat (meat/fish/ poultry/eggs)	Bread/Cereal	Fruit/ Vegetables	Dairy/Milk	Junk Food

Today I ate: (Put foods into correct category)

Meat (meat/fish/ poultry/eggs)	Bread/Cereal	Fruit/ Vegetables	Dairy/Milk	Junk Food

Is It a Good Snack?

Directions:

Circle the healthy snack choices.

Put an X on unhealthy snack choices.

Popcorn

Hot dog

Pretzel

Cookies

Carrots

Candy

Apples

Sundae

My favorite healthy snacks are _____ .

Today, my snacks were _____ .

Peacemakers respect their bodies by choosing healthy foods.

We Care About Each Other's Feelings

I care about you
Do you care about me?
I have many feelings
You can't always see.

Let's be kind
And think before we say
Mean things that hurt.
Let's find a new way.

Color the pictures that show people caring about other people's feelings.

Helping

Listening

Sharing

Calling Names

Directions for Mask:

Cut out I-Care Cat's head. Paste onto a paper plate.
Cut out eye holes. Glue a popsicle stick to bottom of mask.
Get help if you need it.

SPO–1

Directions for Animation:

Cut on the dotted lines. Keep pages in order. Staple on the left side to make a booklet. Flip the pages quickly. What do you see?

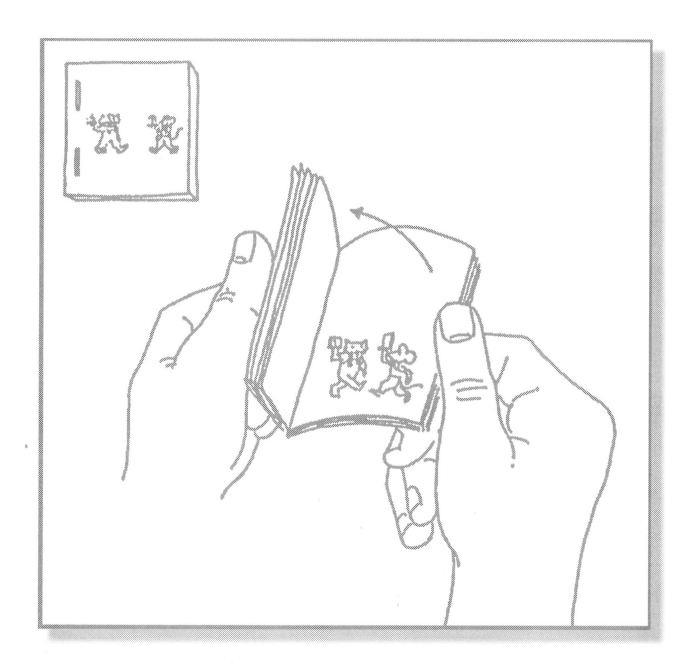

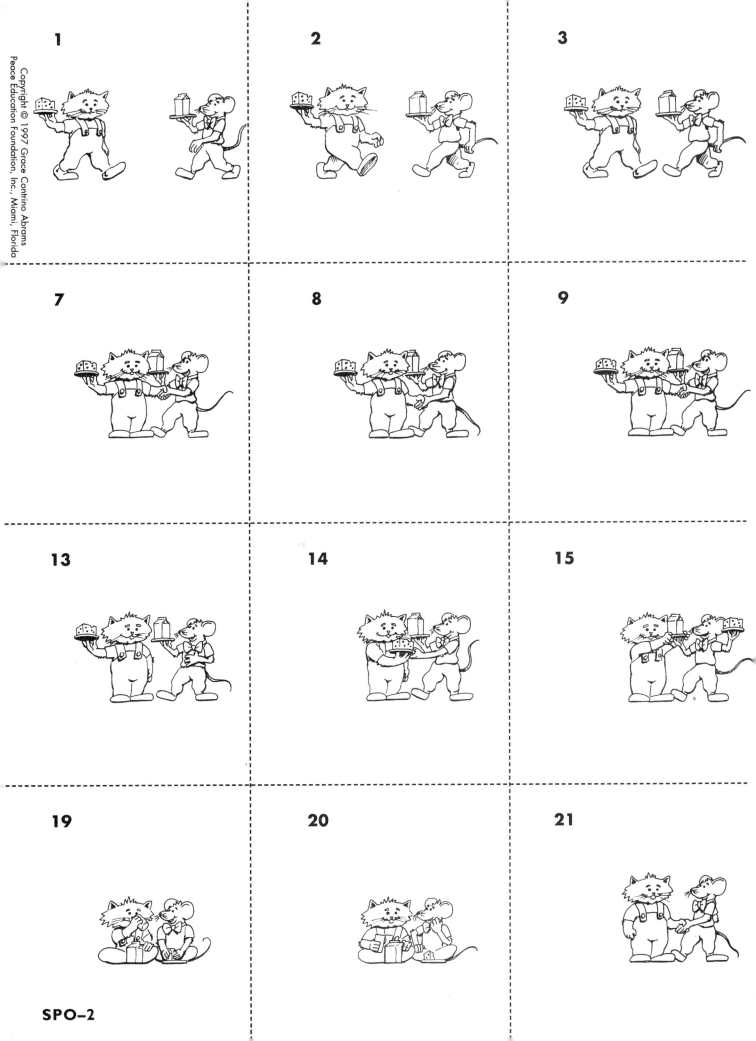

1

2

3

7

8

9

13

14

15

19

20

21

SPO–2

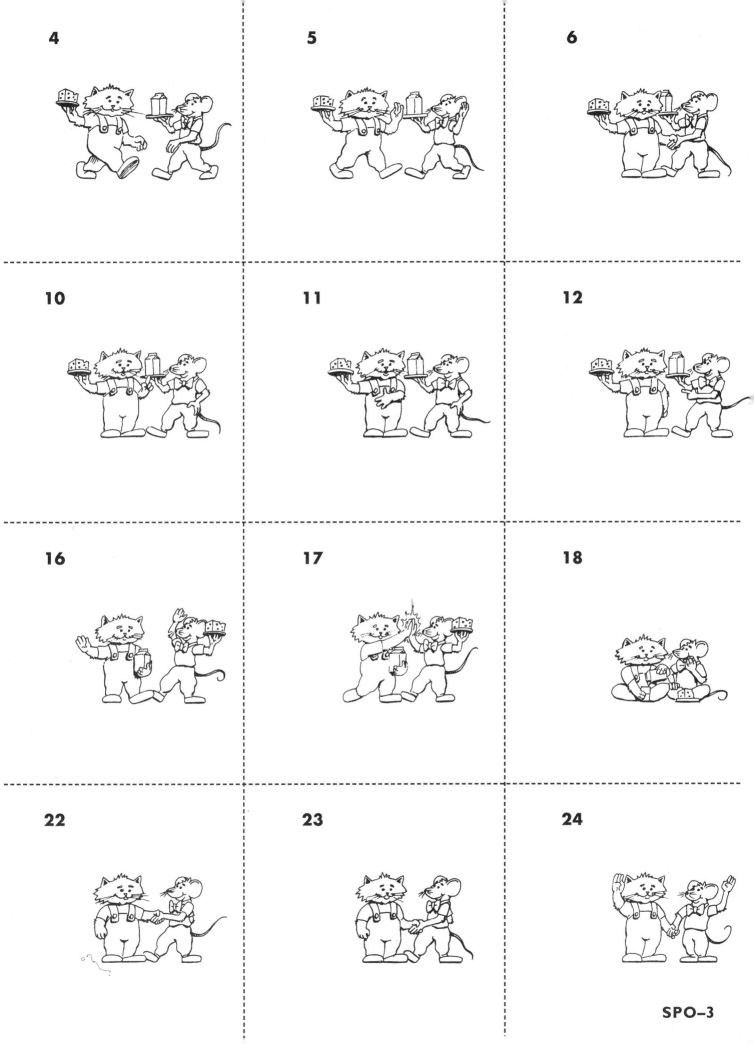

SPO-3

I-Care Rules

1. We listen to each other.

2. Hands are for helping, not hurting.

3. We use I-Care Language.

THANK YOU!

4. We care about each other's feelings.

5. We are responsible for what we say and do.

My Feelings Count, Too

Complete each sentence telling how you feel.

It's my birthday.
I feel _____ .

Someone calls me a bad name.
I feel _____ .

Someone takes my favorite toy.
I feel _____ .

The other children won't let me play.
I feel _____ .

Someone hits me.
I feel _____ .

I share something with a friend.
I feel _____ .

I see a scary movie.
I feel _____ .

Peacemakers care about each other's feelings.

What Makes Me Angry?

I feel angry

I feel sad

Sometimes I get

So DOGGONE MAD!

I want to SCREAM!

I want to SHOUT!

I want to PUNCH

My feelings out!

Tell what makes you angry.

Some things that make me a LITTLE angry are:

_____

_____

Some things that make me VERY angry are:

_____

_____

Some things that make me BOILING MAD are:

_____

_____

What Can I Do?

It is okay to get angry. It is **NOT** okay to hurt people. When I am angry it is important that I find some safe ways to deal with my anger.

Instead of screaming or punching I will

And if that does not work, I will

Peacemakers deal with anger without hurting themselves or others.

When You're Afraid

Circle the items that can hurt you.
Put an "X" on the items that can only
hurt you in your imagination.

Ghosts

Wasp nests

The dark

Monsters

Fire

Lightning   **UFOs**

Being alone

Scary TV shows

Strangers

Mean dogs

When You're Afraid, Make a Plan

When I'm afraid, I can:

1. _____

_____

2. _____

_____

3. _____

_____

Draw Real Fear.

Draw Pretend Fear.

I CARE!

Peacemakers face their fears with courage.

I-Care Language

A conflict does not have to end with people feeling angry.
We can learn to solve conflicts in a peaceful way.
We can use I-Care Language.

1. I say the person's name.

2. I tell how I feel.

3. I tell what they did to make me feel that way.

4. I say what I want them to do.

> Jose,
> I feel angry
> when you push in front of me.
> I want you to go back in line.

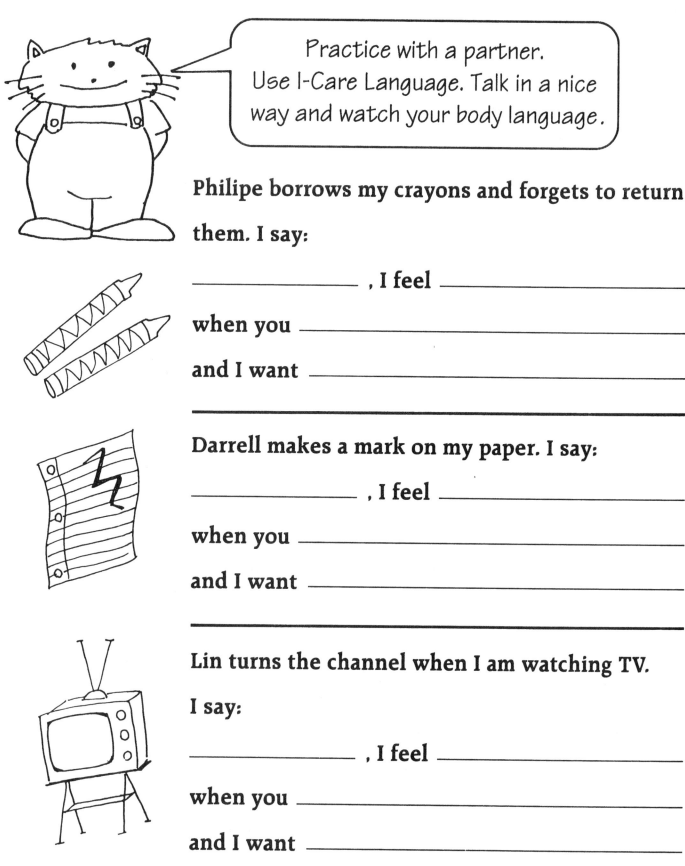

Practice with a partner. Use I-Care Language. Talk in a nice way and watch your body language.

Philipe borrows my crayons and forgets to return them. I say:

_____ , I feel _____

when you _____

and I want _____

Darrell makes a mark on my paper. I say:

_____ , I feel _____

when you _____

and I want _____

Lin turns the channel when I am watching TV. I say:

_____ , I feel _____

when you _____

and I want _____

Peacemakers use I-Care Language to tell how they feel and what they want.

We Are Responsible

Jane and Jim have a problem. The problem is

_____

_____

_____

_____

For What We Say and Do

To solve this problem as peacemakers they can remember to:

- ❤ Listen to each other.
- ❤ Care about each other's feelings.
- ❤ Use their hands for helping, not hurting.
- ❤ Use I-Care Language.

Then, Jane and Jim can

_____

_____

_____

 **Peacemakers are responsible for what they say and do.**

PLAYING FAIR STRATEGIES

I can learn some strategies to help me when I have a conflict.

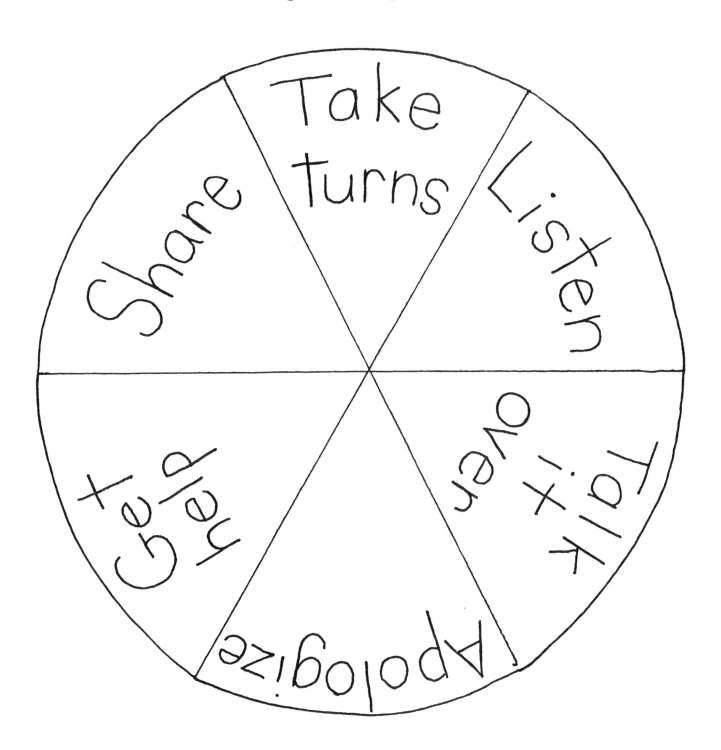

Pick a Strategy

that will help solve each conflict fairly.

When something bad
Makes me sad,
Or when I get angry,
Really mad,
I have much to lose.

What can I do?
Say something,
Do something,
Try something new.
I have to choose!

Peacemakers learn strategies to solve conflicts fairly.

CHANCE SHOWS WHO GOES

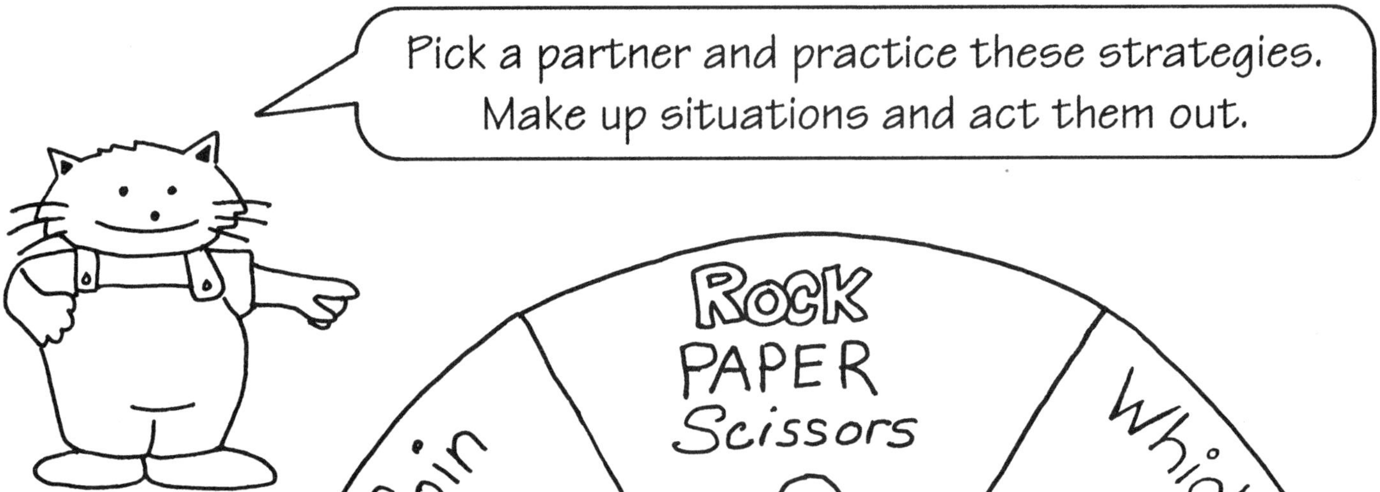

Pick a partner and practice these strategies.
Make up situations and act them out.

Rock PAPER Scissors

Which Hand?

Flip a Coin

Odds & Evens

Who gets the short straw?

Hands on the bat

Directions for Maze:

I-Care Cat and Mouse are having a conflict. Help them solve their problem by drawing a path through the maze, using I-Care Rules. Then, write, draw or tell a story about the conflict and how I-Care Cat and Mouse solved it.

THE PEACE TABLE

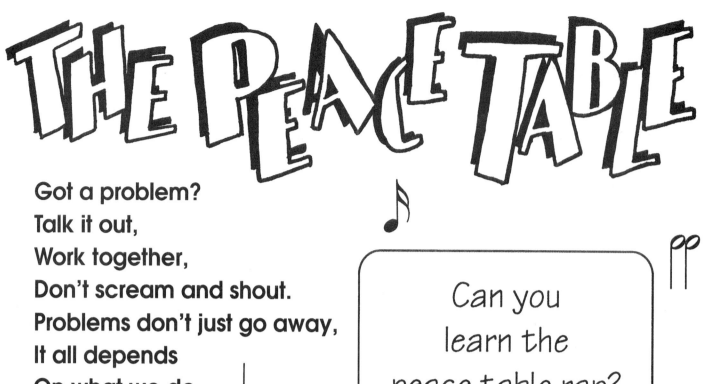

Got a problem?
Talk it out,
Work together,
Don't scream and shout.
Problems don't just go away,
It all depends
On what we do
And say.
Tell what happened,
Say what's true.
Listen to the other
Point of view.
Be polite,
Don't name-call or fight.
Getting even
Just isn't right.
List ideas,
Things that will work.
Say sorry if needed,
Or fix what we broke.
Find a solution
That we both can do,
Try to find one
That fits me and you.

Can you learn the peace table rap?

The Peace Table is a place where we talk about conflicts without fighting or hurting feelings.
We both are responsible for solving the conflict.
We find solutions that we both know are fair.

Tell what happened and how Tom and Bob feel. Tell how they can solve the conflict at the peace table.

PEACE TABLE RULES
1. TELL THE TRUTH.
2. LISTEN WITHOUT INTERRUPTING.
3. NO NAME CALLING OR BLAMING.
4. LIST IDEAS TO SOLVE THE PROBLEM.
5. CHOOSE THE BEST SOLUTION.

Peacemakers go to the Peace Table when they need to.

WE HAVE CONFLICTS

Lori and Glenn were playing checkers. Lori was winning.
As Lori jumped Glenn's checkers he became angry.

Glenn pushed the checker board and knocked down all the checkers.
Lori yelled at Glenn and called him names.
Glenn yelled back and said some mean things.

Lori and Glenn need help. Write in the words that will help them be peacemakers.

Remember to have them tell what happened, how they feel, and some ways they can solve the conflict so that it doesn't happen again.

Peacemakers use the Peace Table rules to solve conflicts.

MEET SOME

Johnny Chapman loved nature. He loved being outdoors. He wanted to do something very special with his hands to show how he loved all life on Earth. Everywhere Johnny went he planted apple seeds. He made friends with the farmers and the Indians. Soon, he was called Johnny Appleseed.

Draw a picture of these peacemakers doing peace work.

PEACEMAKERS

Jane Addams cared about poor people. She bought Hull House so that people would have a place where they could learn sewing and cooking. It also had a day care center so that mothers could leave their babies when they went to work. She started the first free playground in America. She got garbage trucks to collect garbage. Jane Addams did not like war. She worked hard for peace. She was the first woman to receive the Nobel Peace Prize.

Peacemakers care about people and our world.

I Can Make A Difference

I am a peacemaker

Look what I can do.

To find solutions

I try something new.

Draw
yourself
being a
peacemaker.

Peacemakers know that they can make a difference in our world.

The next time I have a conflict I will

WORD SEARCH

```
X P F R I E N D N V S G Y E
S U O I C E R P V E Z N G S
D I E D U E W U X B T I E A
N O I T A R E P O O C R T E
Q I P P U K T T P C E A A L
T O G E F I R P I M P H R P
L I S T E N U W V L S S T B
H N P J P D S Z J R E Q S P
W I T S E K T O H J R D K Q
V R E P R E K A M E C A E P
Y T I L I B I S N O P S E R
C O N F L I C T D W P T Q A
B U U U K J S O L U T I O N
T N E M N O R I V N E M V J
```

COOPERATION	CONFLICT	SOLUTION
RESPONSIBILITY	SHARING	KIND
RESPECT	TRUST	PLEASE
FRIEND	STRATEGY	ENVIRONMENT
PEACEMAKER	LISTEN	PRECIOUS

Dear Parents,

Now that this workbook has been completed, please encourage your child to talk about some of the peacemaking skills they have learned. These skills will help your child to become a more confident, caring, and responsible youngster.

There are many enjoyable ways to apply "I Care" Cat's rules, which are based on the philosophy that all human beings are precious and deserve to be treated with dignity. "I Care" Cat celebrates the diversity of people while recognizing their commonality. "I Care" Kids treat everyone, including themselves, fairly and with respect.

Good communication skills build confidence.

Encourage your child to talk about experiences, feelings, and ideas. Develop good listening skills by having them repeat stories, songs, directions. Take time to listen without interruption or criticism. Your patience will build trust.

Practice "I Care" language with your child. Sensitivity to needs (theirs and others) will grow. Most importantly, they will gain the courage to speak up clearly and non-violently for what is fair. Congratulate your child when you hear them using "I Care" language.

Feelings, even bad feelings, are OK.

Children get angry easily because they lack the communication and problem solving skills they need to deal with frustrating situations. Discuss your child's feelings, especially when they seem distressed and angry. Read stories that deal with anger, sadness, frustration, guilt (see bibliography). Encourage your child to talk, write and draw about feelings. Reassure them that all feelings are natural and everyone has them. Help your child develop sensitivity towards the feelings of others.

Problem solving skills take lots of practice.

Help your child develop a plan to deal with frustrating situations. Here is a technique that works wonders! Have them close their eyes and imagine a large video screen inside their head. Have them picture the situation like a video. When they get to the point of frustration, stop the "old" video and change the ending. The more they practice new "I Care" endings, the easier it will be to give up old habits.

Everyone has conflicts. Conflicts do not have to end with hurt feelings or violence. Encourage your child to attack the problem instead of the other person. Remind your child that everyone in a conflict has a different point of view, but they all have one thing in common - a desire to solve the problem. By listening carefully and trying to understand the other person's feelings, they can work together to solve the problem.

Create a peace table. A peace table can be any table. It's a place where your children can talk over and solve their problems by themselves. If children need help to solve a problem, any family member may mediate. A mediator does not judge, take sides or give the children the solution. Tell the children there will be no name-calling, blaming, or hitting. The object of mediation is to solve problems so that they don't occur again, and not punishment.

- Have each child tell their side of the story, without interrupting.
- Repeat back what you heard to be sure you understood what they said.
- Ask how they feel about the situation.
- Ask them to think of all the ways that the problem can be solved.
- Have them pick the solutions that will work for both of them.

Be sure that each child takes responsibility to carry out their part of the agreement and congratulate them when they solve their conflicts nonviolently.

Hold family meetings. Schedule family meetings once a week or twice a month. This will give all members an opportunity to discuss things that bother them and acknowledge appreciation for the special things that others do for them.

An "I Care" family doesn't need a special time.

Enjoy your child. Let daily routines - cooking, shopping, cleaning, driving - be a time of fun, trust, sharing, and growing responsibility. Work together as a family. Set up experiences which encourage your child to cooperate. Let family members know you love them and care about them. This is the gift of love.

Books for Parents and Teachers

Azerrad, Jacob. *Anyone Can Have a Happy Child: The Simple Secret of Positive Parenting*. New York: M. Evans, 1980.

Buscaglia, Leo F. *Living, Loving, & Learning*. Thorofare: C.B. Slack, 1982.

Crary, Elizabeth. *Kids Can Cooperate: A Practical Guide to Teaching Problem Solving*. Seattle: Parenting Press, 1984.

Fugitt, Eva D. *"He Hit Me Back First!": Creative Visualization Activities for Parenting and Teaching*. Rolling Hills Estates: Jalmar Press, 1983.

Fry-Miller, Kathleen M., and Judith A. Myers-Walls. *Young Peacemakers Project Book*. Elgin: Brethren Press, 1988.

Ginott, Haim G. *Between Parent and Child: New Solutions to Old Problems*, *New Ed.* London: Staples P., 1969.

Gordon, Thomas. *Parent Effectiveness Training: The No-Lose Program for Raising Responsible Children*. New York: P.H. Wyden, 1970.

Haggarty, Brian. *Nurturing Intelligences: A Guide to Multiple Intelligences Theory and Teaching*. Menlo Park: Addison-Wesley Pub. Co., 1995.

Janke, Rebecca Ann, and Julie Penshorn Peterson. *Peacemaker's A,B,C's for Young Children*. St. Croix, Minnesota: Growing Communities for Peace, 1995.

Katz, Adrienne. *Naturewatch: Exploring Nature with Your Children*. Reading: Addison-Wesley Pub. Co., 1986.

Kohn, Alfie. *No Contest: The Case Against Competition*, *Rev. Ed.* Boston: Houghton Mifflin, 1992.

Kreidler, William J. *More Than 200 Activities for Keeping Peace in the Classroom*. Glenview: Scott, Foresman., 1984.

Lazear, David. *Seven Ways of Knowing*. Palatine, Illinois: Skylight Pub., 1991.

New Games Foundation. *The New Games Book. Ed. Andrew Flugelman*. Garden City: Dolphin Books, 1976.

Lazear, David. *Seven Ways of Knowing*. Palatine, Illinois: Skylight Pub., 1991.

Prutzman, Pricilla, Lee Stern, M. Leonard Burger, Gretchen Bodenhamer. *The Friendly Classroom for a Small Planet*. Philadelphia, Pa.: New Society Publishers, 1988.

Schmidt, Fran, and Alice Friedman. *Fighting Fair for Families*. Miami: Grace Contrino Abrams Peace Education Foundation, Inc., 1994.

Smith, Charles A. (Ph.D.). *The Peaceful Classroom 162 Easy Activities for Teaching Preschoolers Compassion and Cooperation*. Mt. Ranier, Maryland: Gryphon House, 1993.

Sobel, Jeffrey. *Everybody Wins: 393 Non-Competitive Games For Young Children*. New York: Walker, 1983.

Tiedt, Pamela and Iris Tiedt. *Multicultural Teaching: A Handbook of Activities, Information, and Resources*. Needham Heights, Massachusetts: Allyn and Baron, 1990.

Books to Share With Your Child

Aliki. *Feelings*. New York: Greenwillow Books, 1984.

Aliki. *We Are Best Friends*. New York: Greenwillow Books, 1982.

Aliki. *The Story of Johnny Appleseed*. New York: Simon and Schuster
 Books for Young Readers, 1988.

Browne, Anthony. *Willy the Champ, 1st American Ed*. New York: Knopf,
 1985.

Burns, Marilyn. *I Am Not a Short Adult!: Getting Good at Being a Kid*.
 Boston: Little, Brown, 1977.

Carlson, Nancy L. *Loudmouth George and the New Neighbors*. Puffin
 Books, 1986.

Crary, Elizabeth. *I Can't Wait. A Children's Problem Solving Book, 2nd ed*.
 Seattle: Parenting Press, 1996.

Crary, Elizabeth. *I Want It. A Children's Problem Solving Book, 2nd ed*.
 Seattle: Parenting Press, 1996.

Delton, Judy. *I Never Win!*. Minneapolis: Carolrhoda Books, 1981.

Demuth, Patricia. *Max*, *The Bad Talking Parrot*. New York: Dutton
 Children's Books, 1990.

Keats, Ezra Jack. *Goggles.* New York: Aladdin Books, 1969.

Lionni, Leo. *Alexander and the Wind-Up Mouse*. New York:
 Knopf/Pantheon, 1974.

Lionni, Leo. *Fish is Fish.* New York: Pantheon, 1970.

Lionni, Leo. *The Alphabet Tree*. New York: Pantheon, 1968.

Richter, Betts. *Something Special Within*. Marina del Rey, California: DeVorss, 1982.

Rogers, Fred. *If We Were All the Same*. New York: Random House, 1987.

Simon, Norma. *I Was So Mad!*. Chicago: A. Whitman, 1974.

Spier, Peter. *People*. Garden City: Doubleday, 1980.

Surowiecki, Sandra. *Joshua's Day*. Durham: Lollipop Power, 1977.

Thomas, Marlo. *Free To Be—A Family*. Toronto: New York: Bantam Books, 1987.

Viorst, Judith. *Alexander and the Terrible, Horrible, No Good, Very Bad Day*. New York: Atheneum, 1972.

Wells, Rosemary. *Shy Charles*. New York: Dial Books for Young Readers, 1988.

Wilhelms, Hans. *Let's Be Friends Again*. New York: Crown, 1986.